6/09

Map of the Lost

MARY BURRITT CHRISTIANSEN POETRY SERIES
V. B. PRICE, SERIES EDITOR

Also available in the University of New Mexico Press
  Mary Burritt Christiansen Poetry Series:

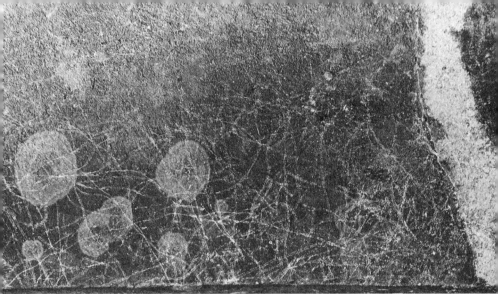

Map of the Lost

Miriam Sagan

University of New Mexico Press | Albuquerque

© 2008 by the University of New Mexico Press
All rights reserved. Published 2008
Printed in the United States of America

14   13   12   11   10   09   08   1   2   3   4   5   6   7

Library of Congress Cataloging-in-Publication Data
Sagan, Miriam, 1954–
    Map of the lost / Miriam Sagan.
        p. cm. — (Mary Burritt Christiansen poetry series)
    ISBN 978-0-8263-4160-0 (ALK. PAPER)
1. New Mexico—Poetry. I. Title.
    PS3569.A288M37 2008
    811'.54—dc22
                2007036651

Book and jacket design and
    type composition by Kathleen Sparkes
This book was typeset using Warnock Pro OTF 9.5/12
Display type is Helvetica Neue

Contents

Foreword

You are never completely lost if you have a map of where you've been. A map is not a terrain, of course. It won't help you find your way, unless you know where you are. When you map the landscape of your life, you're doing what all mapmakers do, putting memory's leavings as precisely as they can on paper. A map of poems is something like that too. Lost in a vanishing world, as all of us are, a poet who maps her search for the future can be a welcome companion on the trail of our own lives. Part pathfinder, part exemplar, Miriam Sagan knows where she comes from and where she is. The past is as gone as the future is unfound, but the traces of mind-lands that remain from our journeys are like spores in the forest. We can use them to track where we might be going. Sagan's search for home in *Map of the Lost*, full of the details and intimacies of the places of her life, confirms for us the advice of Heraclitus to know a great many particulars if you want to find the truth.

Because time is a continuum, memory can foreshadow the future. And in this expansive and wise collection of poems, Sagan says that home "is always the starting point, often literally my house on Santa Fe's west side." The poems range south across the deserts of the world, she says, then off to the east through her childhood, New York, and Europe. Then west to Japan, to "notions of Buddhism," and California. "And the last section heads northwest with Lewis and Clark, then north to Alaska. . . . It is the search for home—not just in place but through history, art, myth, literature, and the self—that is the true map of the book."

Sagan moved to New Mexico in 1984. She is as at home. In a poem called "Take a Left at My Mailbox" she writes of her daughter taking her to an acequia

> . . . full of trash
> Where a sodden quilt lies in the middle of where
> Stream once moved sand
> In eddies. The homeless camp
> Disintegrates, only one mattress left

And I'm lecturing my daughter
Who steps back to photograph it
"Don't come here alone,"
And she retorts: "I have since I was eight," and then
"It's so peaceful here, but
I hate the fence." . . .
From here you can cut
Up behind the Indian School. . . .
. . . We're back
In the neighborhood where my daughter
Immediately becomes lost.
"I don't get straight streets," she says.
My money's good here, I buy two cups of foamy chai
And look in her face, turning from girl to woman,
And want to construct
My map of the lost.

Of a forest fire near the Espanola Valley, Sagan writes of loss in a
way that only lovers of New Mexico can understand.

. . . I can't help but wonder
If it is harder
For a santero to watch the forest burn
As if a crowd of unborn
Saints went up in smoke
Including Santa Barbara, protectress against lightning,
San Isidro who plants the fields with angels.
For the saint is already in the wood. . . .
The faces in the knotted bough
Peer out for those who see them.
Higher up, at 10,000 feet
It's late spring, not yet summer
Where aspens, pale sisters almost leafing green
Seem to drift

Through the pointed firs
Like smoke.

In her powerful homage to Lewis and Clark, "Northwest Passage,"
Sagan gives us a view of how mind cascades with metaphors of place
derived from every place that fits. She follows the great mapmakers

Into a landscape Jefferson imagines
Still young with volcanoes where mammoths walk
. . . the way they might in a mural at the science museum. . . .

Preserved bones scattered on the great dining room table
A magpie and a prairie dog—rare creatures—
Housed in Philadelphia's Independence Hall.
To live by an idea, a signature,
The rights of man freed from superstitious bondage.
Ideas will catch up with us in decades, centuries. . . .

Miriam Sagan reminds us that all human minds are maps of the
lost, great overlays of the details of where we have been and what
we have learned and heard and even said ourselves, and that each of
us, in the mind space that is ours, has the possibility of an unending
adventure of recollection showing us a way to find out who we are.
                                        —V. B. Price, Albuquerque

Acknowledgments

Some of these poems appeared in the following publications, print and electronic:

"Heraclitus" in *Leaf*

"Sack Quilt" and "Rauschenberg" in *Lilliput*

"Hotel Limpia" and "Corner of the Eye" in *MAG*

"The Dyer's Palmprint" in *Wild Violet*

"Writing on the Body," "Jizo Statue. Art Institute," "Tea Room," and "Lighthouse. Cabrillo Point" in *Alsop Review*

"Dar-Al-Islam," "Clovis," and "Writing on Aspen" in *Santa Fe Poetry Broadside*

"Kore," "Quarry," "I'm Looking At Her Too (The Model)," "E-mail from X'ian," in *MGV2* (e-zine, France, in French and English)

"Pluto in Riverside" and "Clothespins" in *236* (Boston University)

"I Only Wanted to Please Myself" in *Zapateras*

"Ana Mendieta: Falling in the Four Elements" in *Gargoyle*

"Elemental Guardian" and "Sitka" in *The Moon*

"Diana Doll" in *Mothering Magazine*

"February," "Die-In," "Emergence," "Where We Came From," and "101" in *Central Avenue*

"Anna Zemánková" in *Frigg*

"Where" in *Santa Fe Literary Review*

"Ex-Voto of a Hand" in *Luna*

"Witch Lights" in *Zia*

"Yellow Calla Lily" in *El Dorado Sun*

"Borrego Fire" in *Whimperbang*

"Dharani of the Return" and "Biblioteca" in *Chokecherries*

"Mid-Life" in *Sin Fronteras*

"Heaven and Hell" in *Bliss*

Thanks to the Lannan Foundation for a Marfa Residency, during which some of these poems were written.

And many thanks to Miriam Bobkoff and Richard Feldman for invaluable help with this manuscript.

SECTION 1

Snow at 7,000 Feet Tonight

White lilacs in the dusk,
Neon signs along the strip
Shine purple like a snatch of conversation overheard.
Girl in the butterfly dress
Runs to embrace me,
My daughter and her friends in the backyard,
A boundary line between them and the house
As if they were already out of reach
At eleven, twelve, twelve and a half.
Sometimes you're sure
We'll leave this place
Eventually, as if worn out
By Malpais, volcanic cones
The earth's bare skeleton.
Sometimes I look at my dirty straw sandals
Worn down especially at the toe and heel
From years of use
With a mood like that
Of a frayed tatami mat
In a country temple
The priest is too poor to replace . . .
Well, what did I expect?
Certainly not to get rich
Following this way.

Take a Left at My Mailbox

Cross Sierra Vista and enter the cul-de-sac
Where the pavement ends
Cross over and down into the acequia full of trash
Where a sodden quilt lies in the middle of where
Stream once moved sand
In eddies. The homeless camp
Disintegrates, only one mattress left
And I'm lecturing my daughter
Who steps back to photograph it
"Don't come here alone,"
And she retorts: "I have since I was eight," and then
"It's so peaceful here, but
I hate the fence."
This is no arroyo cut by rain
But a remnant of man, an irrigation ditch
Now watering detritus, the leftover, cast off, plastic bags, and worse.
From here you can cut
Up behind the Indian School
Past the transformer I didn't even know was there
And come out where there once were tracks,
Now just the runners half-buried in soil.
It's Baca Street! We're back
In the neighborhood where my daughter
Immediately becomes lost.
"I don't get straight streets," she says.
My money's good here, I buy two cups of foamy chai
And look in her face, turning from girl to woman
And want to construct
My map of the lost.

City of the Sacred Faith

I used to walk to the Plaza,
Shop at Mangel's, the discount clothing store,
Buy myself the same skirt in three colors:
Turquoise, fuchsia, black
The only hues a woman needed in this town.
Of course, it's not there anymore
Like the old Sears,
Where my second week in town
I tried to buy an umbrella
And was told it didn't rain enough
For them to be in stock. Sears
Became an upscale restaurant up an escalator,
Then—oh, I don't know,
I never go there anymore.

To get to my house now?
Well, remember where the old bowling alley used to be
On Cordova? Start there.
Oh, we had fun, remember the time
We ate a whole chocolate cake for your birthday
And tried to bowl our migraines off?
Remember the De Vargas Hotel?
It's the St. Francis now. I slept there once;
It was practically a flophouse
With those old-fashioned white metal bed frames
Like a psych ward. It was the time
I took the bus
When the bus station was still downtown
In what is now—who knows
A lamp store? Cowboy hats, or lingerie?
You know, those skirts used to fray,
I'd try to keep them going with hand wash
But they bleached out in this sun.

The mountains don't change,
That lovely angle coming into town.
But we've changed, somehow,
Although it's less easy to explain
Than pointing to what has sprung up,
What has been torn down.

Ben-Hur

Governor Lew Wallace
Sits writing in the window
Of the Palace of the Governors
On the north side of the Plaza.
His wife has written him repeatedly from the east
To draw the shade, the curtain,
As he bends to the light of the oil lamp.
Every ruffian and bandit he has subdued
Might ride past, circling from the end
Of the Santa Fe Trail
And, in vendetta, shoot him through the head.
Pull the curtain closed, she pleads.

But he is absorbed, writing
His epic of Rome and the birth
Of Christ, the story in part
Of a beleaguered provincial governor,
Noble, a general, well-intentioned,
Civilized (and not unlike his author)
Harassed on all sides by swarthy natives
Who speak a different language,
Eat a spicier food,
Worship different gods . . .

An imperial power must take what it will choose.
So render unto Caesar
What is Caesar's—river, fruitful land,
An obedience we never can quite believe.
The Roman governor is perplexed,
After all, he is no fool,
Does not believe the visible is everything.

These restless so-called citizens of empire
Believe some new spirit walks with them day and night.
As to the unseen gods, the governor thinks
Maybe they are right.

Santa Fe Trail Sestina

Writing by lantern light in her diary,
Tent pitched by the side of the trail,
A woman much younger than her husband
Leaves Tennessee, Ohio, to go west,
Sees for the first time, Spanish
Peaks stand sentinel, glowing white

With snow. As a bride, dressed in white,
Victorian mock oranges, lace, her body a diary
No one had written in English or Spanish
Matrimony seemed some kind of trail
Leading to old age, sunset, west
A wife is part of the husband.

He takes her from her mother's house, this husband,
Trader, captain, Indian killer, believes the white
Color of skin entitles him
To take what is west
Won't read the diary,
Of rock, arroyo, mesa, what is not trail
Just as he won't read or write in Spanish.

She puts her hair up, looks suddenly Spanish
In comb and mantilla, her husband
Turns at the ball to a woman trailing
The edge of one finger across her fan, ostrich white.
What will she write in her diary?
Who flirted, whose manners reminded her of the east?

The panes of her house reflect the west.
In childbirth she curses in English and Spanish,
The child born dead. A boy, she records in her diary,
The native women give birth away from husbands,
Wash in the river, white
With ice, wash the child, wash away the bloody trail.

Night led her here, like a trail,
Away from teacups, linens, led her west
To die young, buried in a wedding dress, still white,
Buried beneath guitars singing in Spanish
Leaving other women to her husband
Leaving only the pages of her diary.

Her diary remains, a record of the trail.
Her husband prospered, conquering the west.
In the Spanish olives, a dove flutters white.

Cortez Street

Is narrower, but parallel to mine
To turn into it is to enter
The realm of shabby beauty
Parochial—the jingoistic
American flag decals on old cars
Veteran plates on the truck proclaiming END WAR
Or more importantly—the bare trees, the piñon brown in drought
Afternoon shadows across a fence of sticks
That keeps some things in, some out
And this street, which of all the streets in the neighborhood
Has a feeling of melancholy, and of half-kept secrets
As if its very narrowness
Were about to reveal something.

A left on Sierra Vista
A left again on Kathryn
I'm not immune
Either to beauty or decay
I see my own wall from the corner
With stucco peeling
Plastered years ago
On a too wet day
By my brother and someone named Grey.
And the corner house, the C de Bacas'
Has, in this light
A pink square, faint but visible,
Etched palely on the adobe house
Not the Mona Lisa's face
Or even a pond full of golden koi
But catching my eye nonetheless
Lovely, and meaningless,
Not on purpose.

Demeter in Winter

These seemingly endless days of autumn
On the verge of collapse, but not quite
Time to move the geranium pots
Into the cold study
Out of the first snow.
I've moved from Proserpina to Ceres
From wild heedless girl
To the mother of one . . .

Fog hangs in the mountains
Things are gathered in
A harvest of the past
Memory
Like a bitter taste
Kept me awake all night
Demeter with a hot flash, a cornucopia, an opinion, a grudge
The boyfriend who appears suddenly on his bicycle
Not exactly a Hell's Angel, but still . . .
And underworld, in its bejeweled cavern of dreams
As we traipse along
Past the cold faces
Of lovers who have forgotten.
It's winter, with its mantras
Of earthworms and topsoil
Of compost—rinds, eggshells, withered gladiolas
Ash on the roses against fire blight,
Turning to fertilize the future.
What we feared
We have come to endure.
And count ourselves
Successful at this survival:
Catching the bus
Chopping vegetables
Simmering soup.

Demeter, goddess of corn
Goddess who is grain
Succeeds, if only partially,
In continuing as mother to her daughter
After the kidnapping, or rape,
After the appearance of Death with his horses
Breaking through the surface of the earth,
After hunger
And submission
And eating what you should not eat
The anorexia of pomegranate seeds
Hunger strike
For a mother.
After all this, and a hysterical
Breaking of china and name calling
Which leaves the furrowed fields in snow
Earth barren—
The cell phone rings, the knock on the door
The girl is back
Wearing odd bracelets of skulls
Hair dyed purple
In black fishnet
But back from the underworld, back.

Kore

Snowfall, all night, by dawn
Shapes are rounded
The bush becomes a beast you must beat with a broom
And some oddity in the neighbor's yard
Appears to be a stovepipe poking through the arctic waste.
I was nervous in both darkness and light
Inspecting a bruise, expecting a letter
In a white envelope
Maybe a thin aerogramme from the realm of the dead
On a day without news, when the State was closed
Where footprints seemed more permanent than usual
And I took dictation as if from the radio, or music . . .
Where red finches slipped in and out
Of the thornbush fence
And I wondered
About the unexpected
About who was caught in snares
And who ran free all day . . .
And couldn't make anything of my dreams
And was waiting for my daughter to appear
In a nightgown, a white slip dress
With a bruise on her neck
Love's bite
From a boy I'd never seen . . .

Each Thing Has Its Own Meaning

1.

Brick facade of the gutted building
Window frame sockets, covered in ivy
You have come to believe this world is real . . .

Forgetting the great rift valley
Of genesis
Where story is twisted in a helix

You stitch onto fabric
A tapestry of survival
Quilting the journey

Sisters with braids, the terrible
Appearance of soldiers
Fighter planes across the river

Embroidered beast of the apocalypse
Allegorical unicorn and allegorical girl
Emblazoned in red *mon seul désir*

Or sequined coverlet for the bed
Damballah—snakes and eyes
Who dreams beneath this does not dream alone . . .

    fish of buttons
    fish of bottlecaps
    coins

And on a city street, like this one
Oak tree hung with shards of glass
Reflecting, tinkling

Whose roots go down to Hell
Serpent at its base
Your spine's spiral staircase

    each individual wave
    its individual mermaid
    conveys

Blue perfume bottle
Sequined flag—this retablo that says we lived—
Ridden as vehicle to the other world.

2.
Phantom pain, the brain registers the limb
The arm is there, the way grief registers an absence

Invisible writing appears in the flame
Flash flood in the wadi erases the hieroglyph

First thing in the morning, naked in bed
You tell me of towns drowned by the reservoir

Seaglass, a girl at the edge of the wave
Time at the edge of continental drift

Fog's transformative metaphor
The Polaroid (you, your mother and father) discolored, fading

Jonah and the whale
Wooden story told in zigzag saw

The reluctant prophet, the devouring fish
The shade of the gourd vine, God's feminine mercy

This story is about hunger, but whose?
Anorexia, a talisman against appetite

They call my name to pick up my order
I drink a chai in the square as if nothing has changed.

3.
Path Through The Forest is a quilt pattern—done pink on gray

You might state the obvious—that beauty is about survival

A woman might be named China but never leave this remote hamlet

Suddenly the newspaper that plasters the wall catches your eye

A woman in middle-age discards a husband and finds a better one

In the weaver's somber palette patches of sparkling gold appear

You try to explain the problem to me of loving one person more
    than another

These shoes were inappropriate for walking across time

The box of chocolate was actually buttons constructed to look like
    chocolate

When they demanded the vote the white ferry owner cut off the boat

You can see this pattern in the mind

House hanging from a cloud

Smoke

Rag doll on the floor, then baby on the hip

In time, all this became phantom

Firefly in the bedroom blinking a signal. Aphrodisiac. Fate.

Lazy Gal—that's my pattern!—just stripes, not star or cabin but
    vanishing point

A beautiful fox crosses the stone wall in broad daylight, tiger lilies

Petunias and the geraniums of Africa crammed in,

Pink and white striped morning glories

It was color that found you, and led you out of the thicket

Foreshadowing, that hue of dreams

Heraclitus

It's snowing—fat wet flakes
My sixteen-year-old daughter's head is bent

Translating syllable by syllable
From the ancient Greek

Of Heraclitus, who said the universe
Was, and is, and will be fire

It's morning before the cloud moon rises
In clear heaven's peerless blue

A row of school buses glows orange
I ask myself—what's different, what's the same?

On the radio, after a lifetime
Janis is still singing "Ball and Chain."

Panhandle

Beneath the blue flicker of wings
Blinking neon sign
At the Blue Swallow Motel
In Tucumcari
I dreamed I lost a young girl
At a crowded bus stop in a great city
I woke to unpopulated darkness
All the way to the Texas border.

Original Star. Eclipse.
Names of windmills
Without which these places would remain
Only lightly inhabitable
By those who break camp at dawn
Break down their tents and go
Where the morning star brands the east.

Friendship quilt folded in the antique store
What never was meant for sale
White and blue pieced
Each square autographed
With the embroidered name
Of someone now gone.
No wonder, in this wide expanse
The heart turns to the invisible
Spirits that seem to animate
Our story.

Sack Quilt

Beauty outlives its maker
These patterned squares
Some vivid chinoiserie florals
Like wallpaper in a rich woman's parlor
Some faded to impressionist blur
Like the sea on a rainy day
Sewn on tough pink bunting
Like the plains that stretch away
And can drive a woman mad
Unless she can piece them together

Florence Pierce
Untitled, number 102, 1994
Resin on plexiglass

. . . what comes in across the plains

white space=silence?

a few droplets
a child's finger traces the windowpane

algebraic equation of expanse

how are you doing?

void, empty, blank, open

without footprints.

Hotel Limpia

Line of red rocking chairs—
West Texas wind . . .

You could come here to be cured
Of tuberculosis

But not of the loneliness
That affects even my heart

Sitting in the drugstore
Reading the paper, eating a sandwich

Even I can't explain
What brought me here

Among dry jagged peaks—
What passes for mountains—

Winter courtyard empty
Except for the smell of smoke . . .

Simile

like an orange tree
in a Spanish poem
like the sound of a fountain
in a dry courtyard
like losing someone you love
on an ordinary sunny day
like the red-crested bird
that eats the crumbs off the table
like asking yourself:
what did I expect
like a ruined basilica
seen by moonlight
like falling in love again
with a familiar face
like a stain on the sheet
with no apparent narrative
like the Inca's headdress
of iridescent flowers
like leaning on a cane
in the middle of an earthquake
like learning to believe
it is not your fault
like a diorama of the moon
shooting out of the earth
like hearing in a dream
the Sanskrit word "maha"
like a mosque of white stucco
in Tucson, Arizona
like a Roman statuary niche
like a Moorish arch
like a pot painted with quail
like the profile on a coin
like getting what you want
like a child who can fly
like an orange tree completely covered in oranges

El Copal

In the narrow strip of dirt
Between the wall and sidewalk
Enormous prickly pear and an even larger
Jacaranda like a flock of violent pink butterflies . . .
The wall is red, fading to lime green
Or azure, lapis, or headshop purple
Juxtaposed with yellow . . .
Secondhand clothes are a little sad
But irresistible
The kimono that slides open
Once revealed another woman's
Naked torso framed in the silky flowers . . .
And if you are too poor
For God to give you a cactus
An old dry mop is propped by the side of the house
And on the fuchsia porch
Is a white metal chair
For sorrow, or for joy.

The Dyer's Palmprint

Henna footprints on cloth—
I also went looking for God
In the pre-Sahara, the African plate, the Anti-Atlas mountains
Following Venus above the wadi
Evening star hanging over arroyo.

Neolithic knot
Snake carved on the polished rock
Rhinoceros, gazelle
Before the water left . . .
In the Tuareg alphabet
The geometric letters
First lose their vowels
And then their meaning
For all but the white magicians
Or the women palm printing henna
Who can still spell
Your name, sign of the zodiac
Herbs, minerals, and numbers
An olive tree
The saint's tomb
The medicinal names of God.

The greatest dangers to the cloth
Head scarf or wedding blanket
Are envy and ill-will.
Spit, spit,
Against the evil gaze.

To learn is to remember
The angel touched your lip, too
In the womb
And made you forget
Like Babel destroyed
Or Alexandria burned
The glyphs, the alphabet.

Pentagrams, crosses, stars
Dots, squares, horizon line
Roman granaries fortified
On the fringe of the Sahara desert.
A bride, an apostle
St. Mary of Egypt
Who resurrects the pieces, like Isis,
Who collects the shattered.
Stem cell, consonants, constellation
Eve's footprints in sand . . .

Writing on the Body
    After Shirin Neshat
    artist, Iran/USA

Beneath the veil
A script of Farsi, or Arabic
Written on skin
Nose, cheeks, forehead, chin
In an alphabet that sheds vowels
A dot, a dash, an umlaut,
Your tongue on mine.

It is too late to be unwritten
As if breath had tattooed from within
There is no paper on the ward, in prison
Or in the white-walled room that once schooled girls
Only the words
Written on the wrist
Like a hospital tag, or silver bracelets
Or what the suicide will slit,
Your own name—lest you forget.

Enveloped in latex like a caul
The nude is struggling to be born
The holy book is black fire on white fire
That's obvious, a dominant script
God writes on the blank
But the void itself
Writes on our hearts' silence
White fire of emptiness.

Dar-Al-Islam

All interiors must be Moorish
How else can the mind
Reflect enclosure?
Two plum trees
In full intoxication
Purple blossoms scenting bees.
Off to the east, a long line of mountains
Inside, a repetition
Of tiles, motif, flower
The mind of god must be a spiral.

I'm afraid the door might lock behind me,
Above the lintel
Mud nest of the house swallow
Unsupported archway
Covered in adobe
Architecture as impression—
Bootprint left in mud.

In what book
Did I slice
The uncut pages?
First volume of the unexpurgated
Arabian Nights—
Maybe that is why
This courtyard seems enchanted
An open room
I can neither close nor enter
This is an illusion
Neither veil, nor tent
One moment of bees in plum blossoms
Extends a hundred years.

I Only Wanted to Please Myself

I dreamed Diego Rivera was living
In Columbus, New Mexico.
In the dream he sits in his garden
Behind a high fence of grilled latticework
Painted green. I am extraordinarily pleased
To see him, and pleased with myself, too,
That I've figured out what no one else knows—
Where he is, and that he is alive.
Awake, I make notes in the small
Chinese brocade book,
The jade-colored one:
I write: bullet point:
"I have frittered my life away
Mostly on clothes, and love,
But I mind less
In middle-age."

Dream—my husband and I
Are in a class on sex.
We prepare for our final exam
I look at his skinny naked body and say
"You look like you've studied."
When I wake him to tell him this
He has been dreaming
About the potholed highway in Chihuahua.

I write in the notebook:
Bullet point: "Gilgul.
The wheel, reincarnation
How some rabbis believe
A Jew can be
Reincarnated as a stone."
Bullet point: "Things I Regret I Did Not Buy."

After the dream with Diego Rivera
I realize I must have been wanting
To cross that border
For a long time . . .

Clovis

a digging stick, a tent stake, a fishtail point flint

a cinder cone over a vent to earth's magma core

a pink trailer set among sunflowers

the word FEED in faded red letters on a white wall

to be known by what you leave behind:

chips of flint,
Venus de Milo,
headless Aphrodite
white & naked
in front of a red curtain
at the Metropolitan

a spindle, a spindle rock, dinosaur tracks

a very old man sitting alone at a picnic table

a very blue lake

something happened to the narrative

bullet holes in the white tin ceiling

cloud of bison

caves in Brazil

the footprint of a child pushed back the date of human arrival
    on this continent

a very yellow tin church set among sunflowers

extinct volcanoes leaping like green dolphins

something destroyed the narrative

the Folsom Museum is closed, peeling, flanked by rusted shovels

the train passed

the highway passed

something eradicated the narrative

black clouds of bison

bows that shake

arrows that shatter

Writing on Aspen

Shepherds carved in aspen bark
A record of thought
In the lonely summer camps
Scratched in plump women, crosses, directional
Messages of where they were going
There in the Sangre de Cristo Mountains
In the 1800s, white bark
Of aspens, an endless ream of paper
Pale as the sky
Before morning.

My sister and I
Sat on the Athenian acropolis at night
The ruined Parthenon before us
Rows of bleached columns
Caryatids, serene women, supporting
A roof on their heads
Like so many carrying pails of water
We didn't know
What to do or say
Overwhelmed in the moonlight
Sang "America the Beautiful"
Recited the only bit of Virgil in the original
We knew by heart
Unsatisfied, needing to pray
In some language we didn't know.

Black on white, light
Falling through bars of classical
Columns leading away like a grove of trees
The shuddering of aspen leaves
Green turning gold, littering the ground
Shepherds seeking the valley out of the oncoming cold
Unlined white paper
These words.

SECTION 2

February

Snow, the dark trees, all afternoon
The little girls are playing on the rug

The world outside the window
Reduced to black and white

Practical shapes
Of barn and silo, weight-bearing

What daughters say about their mothers
Mothers about their daughters

It's driving snow
And if we enter it

We seem to walk uphill in wind
Above the town, the county's glittering dome

Somewhere classical by the sea
Maidens carry buildings on their heads

Colonnade of Isis where there are no trees
Columns support unwritten turquoise sky

Not here, where boots and mittens
Pile up wet by the door

The fairy tale isn't merely a story
Narrative itself is a kind of dwelling

Baba Yaga's house runs on its chicken legs
And turns, less abode than a kind of conveyance

There isn't just one word for the sound
Of clumps of snow melting off the roof

And we bear what we can,
Discard the rest in silence.

Pluto in Riverside

The scale model of the solar system
Spreads across greater Boston
Starts with the sun in the Museum of Science
Mercury in the lobby
Venus on the top floor of the parking garage
Earth outside the Royal Sonesta Hotel
Mars in Lechmere's Galleria
Where patrons might sip a cappuccino
Jupiter at South Station where the trains depart
With the romantic expectation of arrival
Saturn in the Cambridge Public Library
With Uranus in the branch in Jamaica Plain
And Neptune—across traffic and congestion—
Rests in a mall in Saugus. We don't really have the time
To spend all day crossing city and crowded suburb
And not in all this rain.
Still, I wanted to see at least one—
Pluto is in Riverside, not that far
From where we're staying—the smallest furthest planet
At the end of the line.

We start at the diner in Waltham
Over eggs and middle-aged conversation
With your old friends, coffee, home fries
Our parents, our children's lives
Somehow eclipsing our own
As if our goal were just to survive
And hold up our portion of the human race
Although a different look might cross a face—
Flirtation, memory of romance or anticipation
There's life in us yet, for God's sake.

The moment passes, pass the ketchup, salt
The economy is tanked, the government. . . .
And do we really know?
And should we stay or go?

We pay the bill, it's freezing
Everyone agrees,
Sure, we'll go see Pluto
In the station, at the end of the trolley line.
It's free, and tiny, this side of the turnstile
I'm disappointed, I'd expected . . . what?
Something bigger than my thumbnail
A potato-shaped asteroid of a planet
Or maybe its moon, Charon
Or some vision
Of its atmosphere at perihelion
A trans-Neptunian object
Hard to see with an amateur telescope.
There is no tenth planet.

Pluto is named for Hades, king of the dead.
As a kid, I liked that story
Demeter and Persephone
The daughter out picking flowers
Long skirt, long hair, picking anemones
Petaled purple and red
Then Hades breaks through the crust of the earth
On his black horse, and carries her down
Into the underworld.

At thirteen, I was waiting to be snatched
Longing for someone bad to come along
Grab me out of my mother's white-shingled house
Where she'd yell
"11:30! Don't forget your curfew!"
Down to Hell I'd go
Amethyst cave, the dead with coins on their eyes
Where blind fish swam through the drip of limestone.
Hades, bad boyfriend, I just knew he was coming
I put my ear to the earth and urged him on.

Half a lifetime later
I dream of my mother's city, this Boston
Its subway lines and trolley
Where I stand on a platform in a vast space
And when the train pulls in I rush to ask
The dark gentleman in the three-piece suit
"Is this train in or out bound?"
And he answers, before the doors swish shut
And the train drops underground
"Everything here is inbound."

Beauty and Violence

Late at night on the east side
Of Harvard Square, we
Had cut across the quad and by the bar
On the far side of the avenue
We saw a cop drag a white boy
Across asphalt. We were trying to cross
To the Hong Kong, where the three of us
Two young men and me the girl in-between
Would sit in the dim unmemorable light
And order pu pu platters
Those savory bits
That arrived flanking the sterno's flame.
But we paused, and one of you said:
"Be careful, don't look
Or they'll get us too . . ."
But I can still see that kid
Bleeding and silent in the blue light
Being dragged by the Cambridge cops
And the three of us poised on the curb
Ready for our next round of betrayal.

Rauschenberg
Estate, 1963
Oil and silkscreen on canvas

Walking down the street—the mind cuts up
Chinatown crates, statue of liberty
Who knew Manhattan was so pastel
Gates of polyglot-radio blaring from an open window
Red letter, a smudge, stop sign, one way
Garbage cans. Florist shop.
The sky, Italian cakes under glass
Skyscraper is not actually collapsing, optical
Illusion clouds rushing by
Who knew that the mind was so pastel . . .

Ana Mendieta: Falling in the Four Elements

this performance is about exile
a performance is exile
which begins on a Caribbean island
ends in Manhattan
when the little girls bury themselves in the sand
they build up big breasts and bellies
plump hips they can wiggle out of
skinny selves
it won't last, the romance of revolution
automatic weapons
buried in the sofa
every child must be an orphan
for the sake of the narrative
so this one is about the body as island
a corpse of mud in the stream
which will disappear
in the element
that is not patriotic
that does not rest
this slogan of water.

adolescent body as boat
woman's body covered in mud
pasted against a tree
didn't I have a mother once?
an outline, a silhouette
"and by real I mean
I wanted my images . . .
to be magic"
or—biography as compulsion . . .
the spirits are everywhere

or are they?
black chicken feathers of sacrifice
on upper Broadway
offerings of tobacco and rum
or maybe the Goddess of the wind
dwells only in her particular cave
etched like the Neolithic
limestone cliffs covered in palm trees
old Mother Blood
carved of unbaptized earth.

branding the book brings hot metal to ash
and why this particular book?
Mircea Eliade's *Rites and Symbols of Initiation:*
The Mysteries of Birth and Rebirth,
on this island, the dead
no longer have navels
it is as if they had never been born
and the language has been utterly forgotten
so drive the burning metal through the paper pages
didn't Eliade say—the person
who leaves the city of her birth
must make a story of it?
so as not to objectify
the draped figure
what should I do—
put myself in this line?
I also was born somewhere
and went somewhere else, is this why finally
all the letters catch on fire?

falling at the rate of a falling body
she descends down thirty-four stories through empty space
lands on a roof, now it is truly silueta
this death which is no rehearsal
but one labeled "suicide" or "murder"
or, in a problem of meaning, "accident"
as if a woman falling
out of a window in the sky
created a problem of sense
as if this death were foretold
by the palm reader
by the police
or simply, at this point in the narrative
by the terrible
weightlessness of oxygen
by the lack of resistance
of this city's night
this air

Emergence

Water olla in the desert with a pack rat's nest
Climate shifts, continents drift
The moon shoots out of a molten core
To hang, luminous image of beauty and return
In all of our skies.
A mound of sand
Faces emerging from red rock
Charcoal drawing on the wadi wall
Speaks of mitochondria
Flesh on the skull
And a double helix unwinding
Out of the African rift valley.

The face is a kind of veil
Wrapped in the gauze of expression
Smile hides what it won't reveal
The face of someone you love asleep,
Unguarded, isn't all lovely
Child can be born with a caul
Good luck, or second sight
Although I've spent my life second-guessing
What my face would look like in the mirror,

All lovers act blind for the moment
Running a finger over the nose and lips
The kabbalists say the depression there
Is where the angel laid a finger on the child in the womb
To make the child forget—
Those words on the back of the head
What was your face before you were born?
Once I asked two three-year-olds
Where were you before you were born
And she said: it was dark and I came out and it snowed on my head
And he said: I don't know.

Elemental Guardian—Water
Erika Wanenmacher
Wood, steel, paint, and doll eyes, 2004

She's blue
From head to toe
Painted with waves
As if she'd swum in the sea too long
Like a child with chattering lips
Whose mother cries:
You'll turn blue.
Things marked by the wave
Are temporary—
Sandcastle, sandpiper print, beach pattern
But these Japanese waves
Painted cresting foam
Mark the body like a scar—a mole—
Tsunami
Printed on her left knee,
The throat chakra.
I myself have lain all day
In the bathtub
Turning the hot water up
With my toes
Watching a tugboat float across the surface of memory
And the submerged Atlantic cities
Raise a spire into air.
Her doll's eyes look down
Into her cupped hands,
A salty wave smears her mouth
Crashes across her buttocks.
In the Japanese print
This same wave
Threatens to overturn the boat
And in the far distance
Dwarfs Mt. Fuji.

Diamond Tsunami

There is a wave
You are not in the wave

You are on the expensive balcony
You are at the Copper Queen in Bisbee, Arizona

You are in the wave
You let go of the child's hand

The wave overturns the turquoise truck
You were so proud of that truck

The wave fills every swimming pool with salt water
There is no wave

The no wave breaks over the house
My body is transparent and you can see my heart beating

The wave is in the mind
The satellite photographs show the islands have disappeared

When I say "you" I mean the three persons of grammar:
Me, you, and everyone else

The wave covers the balcony and the palm trees
Yes, we are in the wave.

Del Rey Beach

—early
November darkness and
Rain slanting to come in off the water,
I duck into a gallery
Of Haitian art
Find brilliant colors
Painted on wooden boards:
Mermaid, mountainscape, cluster of small women
Carrying a large platter
Of fruit on their heads.
This is no Carmen Miranda
But something more serious and succulent
Giant strawberry, huge nectarine, enormous banana
Eden's temptation, and I'm
Half inclined to buy it
As a memento
Of all that I desire
In the tropical dark
Which slams shut at dusk
One palm tree backlit
By sunset . . .
But half afraid of some curse
I don't take my money out
As if I will never
Get what I want
Or know what the name is of this longing
Which smells of the sea.

Some Disasters of Water

Hit a high mark in the imagination
Like that time in Vineyard Haven
At the grocery store as I stood to wait
My turn, ladies behind me
In awestruck tones
Spoke of that hurricane in '38.

It scared me even beneath a cloudless sky
How the sea broke the barrier of Stonewall Beach
Took the house on Squibnocket Pond
And the old lady in the house
Out to sea.

Remember that time we drove along the Mississippi
Driving fast on the flattop
Went to see where it broke in '29
Where water smashed the levee's spine
And took away so much
People had thought belonged to them.

Or the ark stranded dry on Mount Ararat
Or the pleasure boats on sand when the tsunami recedes
Or how once in this very desert
Low cambrian seas followed the moon
With prehistoric camels and fossilized palm trees
Or memory, where time converges with space:
An oasis in our dry place.

What I Saw

At that first beach house in childhood
Where the pump banged so loudly
We thought it was a burglar
And an enormous green hornet
That no grown-up would remove
Hung on the screen door
Terrifying me
That's when I saw the moon come up
Huge and orange
Out of the east
And thought for the first time in my life
"I'm seeing something
Beautiful."

Later, I saw the way the fathers
Looked at the Swedish au pair in her hot pink bikini
The way she didn't look back
But dove instead
Into a thick paperback
With a titillating cover
The Harrad Experiment or *Boys and Girls Together*
So risqué, I could barely wait
To read those books . . .
And the thin wives
Waved cigarettes to the tinkle of ice cubes
On the deck.

That's when I saw
The aurora borealis
Drifting south into our sky
Not complete spectacle, but still
Green and white lights flashing across darkness
And that's when I saw the whales
Roiling, black, blue, so close to shore
And my mother and all of us leaping up and screaming
Look! Look! Look!
That is what I learned by the sea.
That everything changes,
That is what I saw.

Diana Doll

My red-haired Diana doll
Came in the pink and blue Madame Alexander box
In satin shoes that soon were lost,
Lost too her curvy arms and legs
When she went wading in the swimming pool
Created in the sink of the downstairs powder room.
My mother, though, at no small expense
Took her to the doll hospital in New York
From which, discharged, her limbs again
Hung in elasticized grace.
Still, there was a blemish on her face
A patch where freckles had been wiped bare.

Thirty-five years later, she's in my daughter's care
Who loves the tiny yellow checks, the lace
On her best shirtwaist dress as much as I did.
"You must have cut her hair,"
My daughter says, and laughs
At a bald spot behind the carrot bangs.
One night Diana is left carefully on a pillow
On the floor of a friend's room;
The ferret, who is allowed to roam,
Bites Diana's soft rubber upper arm
Leaves an imprint of tiny teeth like death.
My daughter weeps, then gathers up again unspoken
This doll named for a pure moon goddess
Who shows us what is loved when broken.

Séance

I don't know what it is about girls at puberty
That suddenly calls the spirits of the dead
By Ouija board or séance at the sleepover.
Chanting "hair on a dog" we could lift
Even the plumpest of our clique
On just our outstretched fingertips.
Yes, it was weird
Suddenly light as a child
Our friend almost seemed to levitate
Ceilingward.
We slept at Jay's house
Totally unsupervised
Decrepit house with blood-red turrets.
At every séance only tried
For one spirit—Lee Harvey Oswald
Please don't ask me why
For I don't know why
We didn't want Cleopatra, Joan of Arc, or JFK
Just an assassin, dead outlaw at that.
Why did we, who went to an all girls' school by day
Think a paid killer
Would leave the afterworld
To talk to a girls' slumber party in New Jersey?
And yet we chanted:
"Light as a hair on a dog"
And asked advice on boys
A yes, a no
From Lee Harvey Oswald.

What I Know About You

1. The Third Person

She crosses the avenue
Feet in Capezios, thin soles against hot asphalt
The man who sells
Slivers of roast lamb wrapped in pita
Sharpens his huge double set of knives
Winks at her
Crossing Broadway, waiting for the WALK sign to flash
In the heat she is sweaty
From hours of modern dance in a closed room
Being what—a sunflower, peace, a breeze
In her dusty leotard.
Walking east towards Chelsea
Uninspired brownstones
Not yet worth a great deal of money
A truck driver whistles
She gives him the finger
Buzzes at the apartment
He calls down: come on up, from the dormer window
He'll be naked in the heat
Cooking something—
What does he do
Until 4:30 p.m. when she arrives?
Her lover, not a boyfriend,
Though others would see a skinny eighteen-year-old
With hair that sticks straight up
With an addled expression of innocence
The kind of boy

One wouldn't fear
To pick up hitchhiking.
But she fears him a little
Hates him a bit as well
For despite the passion of his kiss
The meal he has cooked in the heat
He will never say the words:
I love you.

2. The First Person

I look in the mirror and ask you to zip my blue dress
The dress is both slinky and modest
So it satisfies both me and my mother
It is of some soft shiny material spangled with tiny white flowers
Thirty years later I will remember it
And you won't
I am seventeen and this dress
Looks like hundreds of dresses I will acquire
Throughout the course of my life.
You zip the back,
In the mirror, we look like a couple,
We are on our way to a Mostly Mozart concert
With tickets from my father
You will remember exactly what pieces were played
But not my dress.
I drape a strand of white beads around my neck
Feel both sophisticated and claustrophobic.

3. The Second Person

And now I see you coming towards me from a great distance
You shine with the blue and gold of a lost afternoon
The glamour of memory
As if I had always known you
As if you were my first love
As if your naked body in my bed resisted time
As if the sandpipers we saw on the sandbar
Who left tiny prints washed by the next wave
Were still alighting and flying off
As if the wind knew our middle names.
The name that doesn't change, that is buried
In the parenthesis between given and family
As if it was your face in the mirror
Looking over my shoulder
Both young and old—you.

Inheritance

There have been bandits since the world began.
A chair sits on the lawn at the abandoned hot springs.
Map of eastern Europe, 1938–1939.
White things. A letter. Her forehead.

Certainly rape gave my face its Polish shape;
Jews will eat black bread and Russians shav.
Message encoded in a stone.
Fog. Suicide. Train station.

Bad genes calcify the sinews of my hand,
Bad men—what other kind of men ride through . . .
Dreams of golden fields
It is our border on the map that burns.

Hotel Europa—you must stay or go
Ottoman seaport or a kiosk stand
My eyes are green in the light of departure
There have been bandits since the world began.

Anna Zemánková
1908–1986
Czech. Outsider Artist

Born in an eastern place that can be broken
And will be—where childhood
Fairies hang upside down in bellflowers
And soldiers
Tramp through in boots that speak another language
First one conqueror and then another
Taking the city with its old quarter of golems
Everyone has left but the young housewife
Who begins to embroider pillows and stuffed handbags.

In a place where the only beauty
Is the flowers of the public squares
She stitches on crumpled paper
Paints and crewels the page
These are the private flowers—
Very red—open-throated blossoms
Extraterrestrial—beneath a sky of sputniks.

Can this, or anything else, be explained by its narrative?
Or by appearing to do two things at once
Such as sweep—which is a kind of separation—
And hide behind a mask?
Appliqué a hat, a lampshade
Crochet a whole new story.

The room divider includes silk thread
A mysterious graph, red beads
Five hysterical flowers
Tied together in a knot—this must be madness—
And is untitled
Like everything else in this world
Where something was trying to eat us alive
Before we adorned it.

Quarry

Lava cooled in pillows,
Interstitial space,
Gypsum, smoky quartz
Basalt in the shallow lake
Precambrian marble
Zircon and zinc
Traprock quarry
With houses built over it.

Four quarries beneath the city of Newark
Glacial incursion
There is another city
Beneath the still surface
With amethyst turrets
And transparent gravestones
Crystals into which one could look
And see the future
Which is also the past.
Crystal refracts light
By design, by destiny
Here the bride floats over the chimneyed rooftop
The city burns into a handful of ash.

A quarry is—prey
Rock
Empty pit
The water's surface
Where children pause to dive
Into the green water.

Things have been set in motion that must resolve in flame.
Karma means cause and effect.
You wear this narrative like an heirloom locket.

Where We Came From

Location of the village
Marked on the copied map
Mentioned in the letter
Variant spellings
On the edge of Bessarabia, Ukraine—
Border land.

The dying astronomer
Dictates a note to my father
The disease has recurred
But he is optimistic
This is no star map
No pattern of radio telescopes
Listening to the past
Rather some dot which defines us
Which has been erased.

Destroyed by the officer
Who notes in his letter
"The Jews have been exterminated"
    if I flew across the pit
    I flew on the merit of my ancestors
    lifted on the wind of their coattails.
Grass grows there still.

Where
   Acrylic on canvas, 1960
   Morris Louis

The painter dreams about color,
Color poured on canvas,
A monsoon in the parking lot.
The painter dreams of the rooftops of Manhattan,
Water towers, shacks perched on apartment buildings,
Jumble of vents, pipes, exhaust, tar beach . . .
The painter dreams of a cactus in a pot
On the oilcloth of his mother's kitchen
A red the color of rose madden on prickly green.

Color enters the painter's body
As smoke enters his lungs,
As division entered his cells.
He is too weak to paint.
The machine shoots a cobalt ray into his chest,
Blue, what is this blue to him
Who was the master of the spectrum?
It is raining outside the midtown hospital
It is raining on the canvas.

The colors are a veil unfurling
And he hasn't painted images in thirty years.
The images are in his dreams—
A New York florist's shop in the rain,
Crammed with the color of petals,
Gladioli, roses, carnations—

The pink and white striped kind—
And the smell of flowers
And the cold air
And the humid city outside
And the tinkling bell
As you go from one place
To the next.

SECTION 3

Story. Rock.

Sweep of sandstone
On which passersby have written
A circle, a ripple that might be snake or water
Old petroglyphs, then Ute or Navajo
Drawing of a man on horseback
Drawing an arrow through a bow
Aimed at a bison
At once archaic and purposive.
Handprints, footprints, lots of them
Cluttered, as if meaningful
Imprint of human,
And a Mr. Gonzales
Who wrote his name in 1902
Right beneath it
Another Gonzales, 1954.

Newspaper Rock—so much of my life
Is like this:
The unanswered postcard, the small clay
Skeletons in a dress and top hat,
Blocks painted with nudes,
Cheap shell earrings.
Each thing by itself
Seems to make sense, narrative—
The expired passport, a dead man's pocket calendar, the car title
A miniature book of psalms
In a random collection.

Canyonlands—red rock, green river, cut butte
As far as the eye can see
Remind me of the calendar
My mother hung above the trash can
In her New Jersey kitchen.

A sandstone arch beneath the moon
Captioned "February"
Or the scene from this lookout
Framed "July" or "August."
It's odd, but looking back
I remember most the time I saw the opossum
In the dogwood tree outside the kitchen window.
It clung fierce and feral
To the bare branch
Bright eyes and sharp teeth
Of an omnivore.
It seemed like a message
From whatever lay beneath
The house—topsoil, humus, worms, earth.
It frightened me too
In a way I wanted to be frightened
Like an image on a rock
I couldn't read.

The Folly

Clutter of nations, and objects—
Sacked, stolen, replicated and for sale.
Every day the city yields a tide
Of Mexican skeletons, Moroccan pots, a wooden colonial saint
Draped in a shawl.
At the Cleopatra Cafe—
Which I frequent because sometimes
The owner calls me "sweetie," offering Turkish coffee—
You can buy a statuette
Of an Egyptian cat
In fake faience.

I can't resist the sense of souvenir.
That an object contains the place—experience, memory—
Even a place I've never been.
For ambience is a commodity,
What's real fades as replica
Comes in as icon: the face of the saint
Painted in gold
Is as miraculous as the saint.
And in this destination of immigrants
The Saigon noodle shop,
With its pierced younger daughter waitress,
Its red and gold altar
To the Buddhas of prosperity,
Is Vietnam
And the King Tut special plate
Really all we know of Egypt.

At the corner of Agua Fria and Velarde
Is an ordinary house I pass most days,
With a front yard mishmashed
Like a vision of paradise:
American flags and bunting, madonnas, pixies, flowerpots,
More than one St. Francis,
Naked ladies, pink flamingoes, swans, and cupids,
Santa Claus, a dog, a frog, a coyote,
The Santo Niño, a windmill model,
Snowmen, angels, wind chimes,
And a sign that reads:
"The love of this garden
Reflects the love of Helen's Beauty."
I'm stopped short—Helen of Troy
"When lovely woman stoops to folly?" Then realize it must be
The gardener's wife.
By night the entire place is strung with lights
Candy canes and loops, garlands and strings
That illuminate the grottoes of this corner
Weeks past solstice and Epiphany.

Descansos

Early Street cemetery is dusted in snow
Ringed by a metal fence—you can't get in or out
In that odd quadrant
Behind Tiny's Bar, right near
Where Bonanza Fabrics used to unroll its bolts—
Sentimental pink and blue cherubs,
Velveteen, black and gold stitched spandex,
Red flannel emblazoned with lucky horseshoes . . .
So much is gone from that wedge
Between St. Francis Drive and Cerrillos Road
And the graves on Early Street
Look untended, no bright plastic roses or spinning pinwheels.
Behind them, made dimensional by snowfall
Sangre de Cristo mountains stand sentinel.

The descanso, too, is gone
From the corner of Alicia Street
Catty-corner from St. Anne's
That tolls the time. The descanso was tied to a stop sign
In memory of my neighbor who the cops shot,
"A mentally disturbed man," the newspaper said,
At the end of a long shift, hot holiday weekend in July.
Shot and killed him because he was trying to stab himself
     with a steak knife,
An irony that was lost on no one.
Shots hit him, also a volley
Came through the adobe wall of the adjacent house
Where my friend's redheaded stepsons slept
In bunk beds. They were unhurt
But by morning, everyone was drunk.
I had a shot of vodka and admired
A jungle of pansies, cosmos, petunias in the garden.

The offerings are gone
Time fades to story like an heirloom
A man is dead, a cop on leave . . . the boys are grown
And other things have happened
To interrupt our leafy peace and quiet.

A descanso may be a resting place
For the pallbearers, marked by a cross.
Now is the accident's decorated site
Acreage of death covered in rock piles, plastic flowers
A photograph of high school graduation
A teddy bear, a Christmas candy cane
Even, saddest, that new one
On the east side of Richards Road
With a big stocking for Santa Claus
Emblazoned in glitter with the name of the dead.
Mementos mark both time and space:
This is both the moment and the place
Soul parted from body.
But what about the intersection
Where you should make a blessing
Where your life was saved?
Where knowing or unknowing
You did not pull out into traffic
The drunk passed by, and the police,
Fog cleared, the car skidded
And then stopped, and finally
Nothing happened, and you went on as usual
The route contiguous
Not even checking the rear view for damage.
This prayer is continuous.

Ex-Voto of a Hand

The conquistador bitten by a scorpion
Makes a vow: if he lives
He'll make a pilgrimage to the Virgin.
Recovered, he has a scorpion smithed
Of gold, coated in jewels
To present at the shrine.

So much of life goes unnoticed—
A Hassidic teacher told me once
We might continually recite the prayer
For passing a spot our life was spared
Not knowing what was averted.

In the dust of the plaza
Even at an exhibition
The deer dancers have some power
To stir this air
Sticks in their hands
So that they appear to move
Like the riddle of the sphinx—
On four legs in the morning.
The famous Indian painter
Sits beneath the shade of an awning
Her famous daughter
Is long dead of cancer—
Mother told daughter
She was ill and dying
Because she had painted the kachinas.

Ex-voto means, in Latin, "from a vow."
Even Christopher Columbus
Promised a five-pound wax candle
To the Virgin in a storm.
I'm standing here also
Listening to the painter's small granddaughter
Explain the picture of the koshare
To my daughter.
A woman holds up an umbrella
A conquistador falls to his knees
A ship hangs ex-voto in the chapel
I pin up a silver pair of lungs
You turn with a smile valuable as shade.

Diner

In Colorado Springs, two Valentine
Diners within a few blocks
Tiny deco eateries.
Chuck Stop, painted yellow and green,
Ten stools, one table.
We sat at the black-flecked counter
The owner a talkative, pleasant, middle-aged lady
Originally from Las Vegas, New Mexico
Who knew her diner's history
This was Valentine #654
With a postage-stamp grill.
We enjoyed ourselves
Despite squeezing into the miniscule bathroom
And a few trips later
Tried the other, the King's Chef diner.
It looked like a bit of Disneyland
A castle with turrets
Painted violet, yellow, and Chinese red
It was a folly, custom ordered
By the original owner who had hoped
But failed to use it to start a chain.
This was a numberless Valentine.
As we sat and chatted and ate
We discovered the owner of the Chuck Stop
Had been murdered
Shot in a lovers' quarrel
In cold blood in the diner.
After that, different owners
Tried to make a go of it
But never quite did.
At the King's Chef
We ate much too much chile
Then headed home along the highway

Decided to stop at the Ludlow Massacre shrine
Near Trinidad, which we passed each time
Saying: we really should go look.
The shrine commemorated the miners' strike
Which ended in slaughter, hired thugs
Who burned the shantytown
With its women and children.
The statue showed a family of three
Poised in heroic suffering.
Picnic tables beneath a shady ramada
Were painted red white and blue
In colors patriotic. Something
Was dreadfully amiss, though,
The statues were headless.
Vandals—brash and heedless—
Had come by night and decapitated them.
Pinkertons from beyond the grave?
Local frat boys?
A list of names continued to memorialize
Slavs and Bohemians
Mixed with Trujillos and Montoyas
Whose names also appeared
In such number on the town's veteran monument.
It was eerie out there on the plains
Hot deserted air
Buzzing with cicada sound
And lonely
And lonely
Except for the company
Of headless miners
And everything lost in the story.

Clothespins

Ordinary day—the news is bad, the weather
Fine for January.
Emptying the compost
In the backyard, late afternoon
I see the little white bag
For clothespins on the line
Has finally rotted through.
You hung it here almost twenty years ago
And since you've gone—I've neglected it
Although what exactly could I do
Given how much care
To those insignificant wooden pins
With metal latch springs
Mouths that open and close
Like a need I didn't know I had?
Inside the house, forced bulbs
Bloom lavish red and red and white.
The pins are almost gone to rot
They lie on the ground like bulbs or seeds
That planted, won't grow, only
Disintegrate to earth.
Often, towards morning, I dream of you
Your shape gone
Like laundry taken down . . .
I toss the clothespins into the compost bin
In the evening's east, the moon, renewing itself
Rises like a paperwhite narcissus.

Die-In

We were on the Plaza
Where we rarely go anymore
At the start of the current war.
The kids had walked out of school
When the bombing started
And called us to come too.
We lay down on the cold paving stones
And Talaya danced around
With chalk outlining us.
There were marksmen on the rooftop
Of the Palace of the Governors
It had been more than thirty years
Since I looked up at soldiers
At the moratorium in D.C., where the kid in full regalia
Set down his rifle
Flashed us a peace sign from the top of a federal building.
And this time, my daughter said: they won't really shoot, will they?
And I, forgetting who I was or was with
Said: damn straight they'll shoot
So watch your back.
And now we were lying "dead"
And Irene was singing: all we are saying
All we are saying. . . .
And when it was time to go
I couldn't get up, my bad hip was out
And I needed a hand
To pull me away from my corpse-chalk self.

It felt good to be on the Plaza again
Even lying on the moist cold stones
Trod by tourist feet.
And looking up, we saw the clouds part
And out of the sky, a raptor bolt
A hawk, bird of war
Not the portent we were looking for.

Columns

The old man selling newspapers
Holds down the intersection of Alicia and Hickox
Like a form of punctuation mark—! or ?
He is short and stocky and has
A little dog he brings and secures with a string
He isn't homeless, despite his weathered look
He lives indoors, like us, somewhere off this block
And I see him ride his tiny scooter after work
Or walk the dog . . .

There used to be columns on Baca Street
Two enormous neoclassical ones
At first I was told
They were columns from the old
New Mexico State capitol building
But this turned out to be urban misinformation
Those columns were surplused, or sold
These came from the First National Bank
Originally across from its current location on the Plaza

Parthenon—model of the palace of Athena
In the coatroom in the basement
Of the Metropolitan Museum of Art
I'd peer in . . .
And see the tiny—yet gigantic in scale—
Golden statue of the goddess of wisdom
Of cities, even Manhattan . . .

Ariadne's thread leads to
The body of a man
Head of a bull

The headless statue
Pediment within a cornice
Greek columns—Doric
Ionic—scrolled
Corinthian—shaped like an acanthus leaf
Or Egyptian ones—
Shaped like:
Lotus
Papyrus bundles
Tent pole
Fluted
Palmiform
Capital in the shape of the cow goddess Hathor
Osiris pillars

Colonnades show wealth, power, the presence of the divine
Here it's just wind, snow, apricot blossoms, a cawing crow
I always tell the old man—keep the change.
One Sunday as church let out
You also went to buy a paper
And he asked you
If you could stand in his place
For just a few minutes
And watch the stack of papers.
You did, and then
You started selling them too
And putting the change by for him
As if one man
Could so easily
Stand in another's place.

A tree grew on the roof of my house
Chinese elm with long destructive roots
Grew down into the rotten adobe
Of the portal
Years of heat and drought
Had baked it to dust
And then the snow came, and rain
And the porch fell down
Except where the roots of the tree
Held it up

A good spring for roofers
A bad one for roofs
I've spent my money
For columns of my own
First they lie in the yard
As if ruined in Karnak
And then lifted
They support
Our own quadrant
Of this turquoise sky

Corner of the Eye

I sometimes pass
Those funerals
At the corner of Alicia and Hickox Street
New Mexican families in front of St. Anne church
Dressed in black suits, or sometimes cowboy boots.
I can tell from the expressions
Who has died—often
A very old person, I assume.
The middle-aged cousins look serious but not stricken
And chat, glad to see each other.
Then there are those other clusters
Of the shell-shocked—
Men supporting a woman
Someone's mother or wife
As the cops turn on their headlights
Lead the procession of hired cars
To Rosario Cemetery.

My daughter told me recently
That when she was very little
She didn't realize clouds could move.
Above the preschool playground
The turquoise sky seemed fixed,
A fluff of cloud
Eternally painted on the mountain.
Then, one day, out of the corner of her eye
She saw a cloud move
Looked up, and saw them rushing high
Cloud horses, cloud riders, in the wind.
So we've glimpsed change
From where we stand
Or even merely
Passing by.

Cerro Gordo Canyon

When we washed up here
Inland, from the bay city of fuchsia and fog
At first, we didn't understand
The desert—walked in Cerro Gordo Park
Where terraces from bean farming
Still stepped—and with a wildflower book
In hand attempted to label what we saw:
Found every yellow-blossomed stem a mustard
Every purple flower—a pea.

And we wondered where the sea had gone
In summer's dusk, walked up the road
And found a bank of fossil shells
Smooth and hard, nestled in a trove
In the shale of the cut.
We'd scramble up and pick them out
Go home with pockets full
And lay them out on a table with a potsherd, loose change, the mail.

There was a wind in the canyon then,
Maybe the wind is there still
For although the sea is gone
It might come back
As waves cast foam on the shoreline
Difficult to imagine, easy to design
Just by turning a windy
Corner in time.

Witch Lights

Sure, we saw them once—
Remember, back of El Rito
We'd taken the kids out
To El Farolito, but town
Was blacked out, the grill
Wasn't working, and we all
Had to eat the only thing available
On the menu—burritos.
It was winter, night, cold
Driving back towards La Madera
Yes, we all saw them
Bobbing in the open field
Green balls of fire
As if carried on lanterns
But of course there was never
Anyone there at all
Between the shoulder of the road and the arroyo.
We weren't frightened, not even that impressed
We always knew they were there
Were pleased with ourselves to see them.
All the way back
The two older kids belted out
"Frosty the Snowman" over and over
To keep the baby quiet
Although it was long past Christmas.

Yellow Calla Lily
　　c. 1942
　　Rebecca Salsbury James

Tiny yellow lily
Reverse painted on glass
Might be anonymous
19th-century valentine
Blue with forget-me-nots.
Calla lily shape
Curls upward, coiled like a baby's fist,
Glass canvas seems a window
To the past.
The woman who painted this
Painted so little else:
Two calla lilies in a vase—
A dozen years later
This offering bouquet.
A wife to famous men
Lover to more famous women.
Painting on glass
Expects reversals.
Anonymous leaves no biography
Just a spray of petals
Or these miniscule brushstrokes
Yellow of butterfly wings or a summer apron
Enclosing darkness.

San Isidro

At Spanish Market—
So many San Isidros:
The usual carvings of the large saint,
The small angel driving the little plow,
And the retablos
One of San Isidro with lace at his sleeve
An aristocratic hat, obviously
A gentleman farmer not from here.
And the one we like best—
San Isidro sweating, half naked, looking distraught
As prairie dogs pop up all over his bare field
And the angel appears athletic
Getting ready to plow
So as not to disturb the saint's prayer.
San Isidro had a wife who nagged
She'd rather have a man who plowed than prayed
Went her refrain
But this saint tells us
Prayer is hard work, hat in hand,
Particularly for a saint whose name
Is synonymous with the prayer for rain.

Borrego Fire

Cordova's burning, great pillar of smoke
Rises over Espanola Valley out the Sangres.
Wood-carver I know distantly—friend of friends—
Is quoted in the newspaper
"They told us to go, and we went
There is only one road out
And we took it." I can't help but wonder
If it is harder
For a santero to watch the forest burn
As if a crowd of unborn
Saints went up in smoke
Including Santa Barbara, protectress against lightning,
San Isidro who plows the fields with angels.
For the saint is already in the wood,
Gnarled piñon or twisted juniper.
The faces in the knotted bough
Peer out for those who see them.
Higher up, at 10,000 feet
It's late spring, not yet summer
Where aspens, pale sisters almost leafing green
Seem to drift
Through the pointed firs
Like smoke.

It's Paradise

You water between flagstones
Grow great clumps of flowers
Red valerian filling the treads
All the way down the narrow stairs
From your birdhouse of a house.
Yes, it is troublesome,
Soapwort, delphinium, penstemon
On the steps.
Veronica, flax, catmint, sage
And we-forgot-its-name
Just about everywhere.
You claim
You're just watering the old apricot tree
Whose roots were injured
When the neighbor moved his driveway.
I say—if this were a Chinese poem
These blue, white, pink blossoms
That bar your gate
Would indicate
That as a hermit, you have no visitors.
But I've come for brunch, and eaten it
And now I'm trying to leave
Your yard, flowers decanted.
But there is no place to place my feet.
"I'm just about to prune it back!" you yell.
I know the other name for veronica
Is speedwell
But easier said than done
When it's enchanted.

Paradise Regained

I spent an enjoyable half hour
Listening to women bad-mouth men
Until Catherine, who tends to be cheerful, said:
Aren't they people just like us?
And everyone in Marilyn's living room
Where the autumn light
Caught the paperweights glittering on a glass table
Said: no!

Then, driving along the curve of Paseo de Peralta
I glanced skyward
Saw two enormous pear trees
Completely covered in green fruit
Like dazzling ornaments
And I wondered who—
What Adam and Eve—
Could resist this.

Flea Market

Old artist's box
For sale at the flea market
Smeared half-used pastels
Wads of cotton
Glass vials of color in a wooden case.

Now propped open
Priced at over a hundred
A decorative accent
Like a plate painted with melons
Or an orange glass vase full of tiger lilies.

Beauty can be bought and sold
Can be arranged, go in and out
Of fashion—I imagine
This artist painted blurry scenes
With ominous horizons
Or rocking chairs on a veranda
Rendered with a slight awkwardness.

Lumpish cows in a wavy field,
A sailboat solid on a solid sea,
These images are lost
Quite rightfully gone and tossed.
What remains—the oil sticks of green and gray, azure, magenta
Now commodity
What was ephemera.

Jennifer Bartlett
  Gerald Peters Gallery
  Santa Fe, 2003

Standing still on stage isn't standing still at all
But is dozens of tiny invisible movements
To create the appearance of stasis.
The same is true when the ballerina is lifted
It is not just that he lifts her
But that she makes herself lighter through motion.

Yellow
Painted—a square, a triangle for the peaked roof
Then dissolved
Into a thousand gleaming dots
Pointillism of darkness
Just before sleep
When as a child
I'd stare out from the bed
Try to break up
The visible . . .

Or of course a painting divided into 9 x 9 squares
Or a feeling of restlessness
Very late afternoon
September
The angle of light has changed through the Venetian blinds
A feeling without an explanation
Or narrative

This is what began to interest me
Maybe that is why
I placed three small empty metal chairs
On my writing desk
No more than three or four inches high
From right to left:
Yellow, blue, red.

Abandoned swimming pool
Surface floated with leaves
We all went swimming there naked
There were little frogs, too, swimming
As if in a lily pond.
A white rowboat
Abandoned on the surface of the pond
A loss of control
That had to be explained later
The house
Tumbling down
Into its component
Geometrics
The pond itself
Preserved finally
Cast in metal, sculpture
On the gallery floor
Ripples petrified in rings
Until the viewer finally
Walks away
Out of the field of vision.

Friable

She told me she
Was writing about Mars
And what was beyond—
Super planets, gaseous giants
At the edge of known space.

She said the doctor said
The cells in the lining
Were friable
And then exclaimed—
Friable! I never heard it before
What a lovely word.

She recited the haiku
She'd written
About horses
Rushing from dreams
And for a moment
Couldn't remember the third and last line.

Then she remembered the part about the wind,
Offered me a butter cookie,
A cup of Earl Grey tea,
Remembered the part at the end.

You Left
in memory of ESL

black teacup without a postmark
canceled stamps of tropical countries
a chocolate box full of paste earrings
a tiny book—pressed flowers of the holy land
a raven's wing crossing the page
how you loved paper clips and rubber bands
a quote from Issa—"senseless mystery"
image of two white mugs lying in yin/yang
a dictionary which defines hermeneutics
those faded clippings about angels
how you were a modern poet after all
Japanese wood-block print of a closed shell with scalloped edges
bookmarks
fifty-year-old mardi gras beads
a taxi slows for a mermaid
a snail eats a lettuce leaf
painting of a black sphere
as real as thinking
how most of your teaspoons
were grapefruit spoons
taste of tea and honey against a serrated edge

101

The cerebellum maps the body three times over in its creases
    and folds,
The dream is always the same, and it isn't a good one.
You'd think the hot spring would ease the strain,
No one should use "you" except as a form of direct address.

Your hand is on the doorknob. You murmur to yourself.
Actually, the suspect might be the second person.
You'd think that water could erase the stain,
As if the problem were one of syntax.

Maybe the problem is one of beauty and not of grammar.
The Big Bang is a theory that can be viewed only from the inside.
Space is a vacuum, there is no speech without oxygen,
The remote island strewn with dialects.

Last night, the Big Dipper sat behind us on a hill,
We fell asleep early. Even the kids were tired.
Steam comes out of the earth, sulfurous clouds and rivulets,
Even you and I aren't exactly as we appear to be.

E-mail from X'ian

At first you didn't want to go
To see the great entombed army
Pleading your dislike of tourist sights
Saying it would be just like the photographs
And how the pyramids had disappointed.
As a rule, you go great distances for small things
The very old woman with bound feet
Men smoking and spitting
And you used to write me letters
In clear pen on blue airmail.
Now your words come along invisible wires
The keyboard in Mandarin
The gossip in English
And—did you go just to tell me—
You've seen the pottery army
Partially excavated in its marble palace.
It is like Niagara Falls
Where virgin brides
Woke the next morning and wanted to see
Something vast and impersonal
Throwing itself hundreds of feet down
Over the border between one country and the next.
Something one can send a postcard of—
A tourist can dress
In a replica of the armor
And have a picture taken.
The souvenir is not the train
Which departs the station for the rush of plains.
You see from the window with unimaginable intimacy
People eating rice in the house's upper story.
A cough. The tracks whine.
The earth doesn't yield easily,
Nor does love,
What has been buried a long time.

Dharani of the Return

Seed syllables in Sanskrit
Mandala of the ideal—
Womb world, diamond world
What mitigates between,
A Buddha out of context.
The tortures of hell
Appear on the hem
Of the cosmological Buddha,
The universe appears as if tattooed.
The terra-cotta Bodhisattvas of Qingzhou
Buried in a pit
At Longxing Temple
No one knows why
Cracked by fire and earthquake
Not desecrated
But buried like people, or holy books
Dug up eight hundred years later
Facing forward
Draped in jewels
Flat backed. Gesture of compassion.
The earth is honeycombed with treasure
Honeycombed with light
There is a world within this one.
The hand of the amateur
Copies the Koetsu teabowl in clay
The black raku
Named Mossy-Tailed Tortoise.

These objects speak
Of the unseen meaning in the seen
Like the map drawn by the Mallorcan conversos
Africa in detail, outpost of red tents
South America clear, the North truncated
A map of territory unknown and known
The feeling tone of a place name
And the place—where you sip sweetened coffee
In the shade of some kind of acacia
And call it home.

Jizo Statue. Art Institute

How Japanese
To catalogue
Attributes of compassion.
This young monk
Serves as protector
To women, children, travelers, soldiers, monks
Also to waterbabies
Miscarried, and aborted.
Isn't it kinder
To care for
What we couldn't bear
Than forget completely?
Maybe that's why
I'm in tears
In front of this statue in the museum
Thinking of you
With your shaved head
Even though you died
So long ago
And I grieve for us
As much as if we'd never been born.

Miniature Rooms

Between trains in Chicago
My father would take us by cab
To the Art Institute. There, in the darkened gallery
We'd tiptoe to peer
At the Miniature Rooms
Each more perfect than life.
The tiny pewter teapot
Truly was colonial Virginia;
Postage-stamp embroidered screen—
Victorian England.

This is history. This is exactly real
To my childhood eye.
Cape Cod living room
Has a tea-set tray
Made of one copper penny
A door that opens
To a hazy scene of summer
It's always summer
Outside the snug room
Although years later the book will tell me
The 134 miniature objects
Create more clutter
Than the original.

In these miniature rooms
Emotions are contained
Feeling directed, as in a play.
The world changes, these lighted scenes do not.
Empires fall. Delicate arrangements remain
Like royal dollhouses
A tiny stage on which no actors appear
No children, giant-handed, rearrange.

My favorites are the odd ones out
Gothic cathedral, larger than the rest
Chinese interior, a symmetry of screens
Ancestral portrait, and a teakwood couch
Or the Japanese
Translucent rice paper, straw tatami
Low writing desk, view of a garden
Neither remembered, or imagined
But truly real, closest that I'll ever come
To Nippon
With its rising sun.

Tearoom

In this winter's light
I might be sitting and waiting
Anywhere in the past
For you to arrive and order oolong tea
This might be San Francisco, or Boston
And you—a woman in a dark scarf
Or any man I loved
Turning his hat to the wind.

Every story has its variant
Donkeyskin who flees her father's love
With a magic trunk of gold and silver gowns
Might be some other girl I knew
In her plaid school uniform, gray blazer.
And even Beauty, who goes almost willingly
To the Beast's elaborate castle
Well, there must be something
She is glad to be quit of.

I sit at the small table
In the adobe teahouse,
Snow threatens, then falls.
It's too high, and the wrong continent
To grow tea. Now that I'm fifty
What is my nostalgia for
Lips I neglected to kiss
Or the lips I did?

Akiko

My daughter went to Japan,
Brought me back snapshots and a handful of shells
The size of a child's thumbnail
In a pale pink embroidered bag.
Still, I was so jealous
To hear her say: my Japanese mother . . .
Then the exchange student arrived
Not exactly like a present to unwrap
Or a baby, but like herself
Another fourteen-year-old girl
Suddenly given into my care.

We saw everything fresh—
Our dusty floorboards,
Blue window frames of the house,
Dehydrated sunflowers in afternoon heat.
And between Hiroshima Day
And Nagasaki
She taught us to fold paper cranes
From hot pink, blue, and black origami paper.

I washed her clothes
Hung these small intimate
Foreign but familiar items
On the rack to dry.
She called me mother
And I, who had had only one child,
Called them "the kids."

She wept on her departure,
We cried too.
Mars hung retrograde and brilliant
In the morning sky.
The Daruma toy
Sat on the mantle
Body of brightly colored blocks,
Scowling-faced head,
Figure of Bodhidharma
Who brought Buddhism from the West.
Almost full moon sinking below mountain's horizon.
In Japanese, moon is tsuki
And gekkou—moonlight.

Sayonara Party

After the marimbas play
The Japanese exchange students
On their last night in Santa Fe
Come out in kimonos
And dance a summer dance in the yard

The boy and girl
Who haven't even kissed yet
Lean towards each other
On the bars of the swing set
Seem frozen
As dusk falls, a little rain, then evening

Desire at fourteen
And desire at fifty
Are the same
It is that which is in-between
Which is different . . .

The life of adults with its desire
For mastery, and consummation
Now, though not on purpose
I am back to pure longing

Girl and boy might take forever to actually touch
This is also, after all, what I feel for you.

Biblioteca

If the angel of the library could speak
Or the page torn from the book
Carelessly, or on purpose
Or the little gothic window in the reading room
Or the street corner, or autumn
Or the shiny horse chestnuts in their sputnik cases
Or the red maple-leaf stars
Falling, as if from constellations
Or the Doric column standing sentinel
Or the Etruscan frieze along the edge
Or a warm bay full of dolphins
Or the word you will mispronounce in your head for years
Having never heard it spoken aloud
If the angel could speak
She would tell you only to hush and listen
To the words of the book
Which contain a house with a cupola
A girl like you
Who is also eating an apple
And turning the page.

Lighthouse. Cabrillo Point.

What once was remote—
Coast in fog, sweep
Of mountains into Mexico
Now lets tourists pass
White lighthouse with its small rooms
Victorian and cozy,
Pictures in decorative frames
Composed of tiny seashells, dried weed,
A sailor's valentine.
Kitchen garden for parsley, lettuce, any fresh green
In what was once two days from town.
The assistant in his own little house
Invited to dinner—
But think of the loneliness
Even for the keeper's wife, the keeper, the children
In their tower rooms
Curved, as light is curved.

Mission

Fountain and pool
Full of pink water lilies, golden carp,
Ruined mission that fell in the earthquake
Geometry of the baroque
Squares set into half domes
That California schoolchildren
Must build models of
In cardboard, or with sugar cubes.
Line of great bells
That tolled the hours
To captive Indians
"Conversion was voluntary."
Horizontal line across the whitewashed wall
Native bisection, painted leaves, little birds
Curlicues of color, stylized corn.

On the flat ceiling of the church
Full red sun, blue crescent moon.
They killed the padre here, also at Acoma
Sky City beneath the scudding clouds.
Those first nights of the rebellion
They swung him once, that's all, and dropped him down.
Even today, the young woman tour guide
Won't enter the great adobe church
Each handful of earth
Carried up on a slave's back.

The Dolores, though, runs its green line
Down most of what I crave
From the past. Odd, I never noticed
"The Mission" meant more than taquerias
Those girls on motorcycles.

That the reason I loved it
Also derived from something else.
Avenue of palm trees
Warm enough, everyone said
For escaped blue and green parakeets, pale yellow canaries
That flew their cages to mate, hatch eggs, fly in the flocks
Of the beautiful set free
That place which haunts me
Mission Dolores of unaccomplished dream
Desire for what is lost.

SECTION 4

Northwest Passage

Palladian light, the gracious
House among hills, seeming to roll itself
Like an astrolabe—or the mind—
To mull, and turn things over
Like the meaning of a fossil
A fern in a rock
Put there, but how? God's folly
Or decoration? A sign of majestic mystery?
Or sediment . . . and if this is the case
There's a question about the center of the universe.

Thought is a narrow thing
Confined within a room,
Hexagonal honeycomb.
Nature's God ordains—this arable land
Beds dug in earth
This potable water.
Parquet floor of cherrywood and beech,
Wallpaper of lattice and green vines.
Camera obscura reduces the scene
To silhouette, the epergne
Is a glass tree.
And set by Wedgwood in the foyer—
Enormous antlers
Above a fossil bone.

To place this house within the universe
Cabinets of curiosities might house
Spiral ammonites like the nautilus—
Named for the horned Egyptian sun god
Maps of the world, an Egyptian pyramid
A neoclassical nude
And a narrative robe

Painted by Plains nomads
On a skin. We are here
And then, by effort or design,
A different place completely.

Lewis and Clark head west
With staunch men and a working dog
Into a landscape Jefferson imagines
Still young with volcanoes where mammoths walk
Or mastodons, the way they might
In a mural at the science museum
Today in any medium-sized city—
He looking occident,
We into the geological past.

Bitterroot, where food failed,
Willow islands in the stream,
Red berries on every bend.
The prickly pear in full bloom
Also the sunflower, abundant
Wild cucumber, sand rush, dock,
Sandbars too numerous to name
A fine evening—
Out of the mist, a village
Appears on the bank,
Smoke rises from the lodges.

Preserved bones scattered on the great dining room table
A magpie and a prairie dog—rare creatures!—
Housed in Philadelphia's Independence Hall.
To live by an idea, a signature,
The rights of man freed from superstitious bondage.
Ideas will catch up with us in decades, centuries . . .

Not one man is lost
On this expedition
Except for the burst appendix
Which would have killed in Boston
And later—the explorer's suicide
The rational mind dissolvable
In chemical despair.
We're not romantics yet—this is failure
The bones are a giant sloth's
Not a panther's.

Snow falls on the plains
So deep
The horses cannot travel.
A fir tree set ablaze,
Maps sketched in ashes and sand.
Swans and wild geese
Flying NE this evening.
A piece of scarlet cloth
In the snow, moonlight.
River of No Return,
The corpse of a woman on a raft,
Laced in robes; beside her
Bags of different colored earths,
Her dog, a blue jay.

The girl treks west
Baby on her back
Captured, enslaved, sold in marriage.
By the Pacific Coast
She wants to see
Not just the dead whale
But the sea itself
Great coastal canoe
Carved in wood, images
Of a bear in front,
Man into the stern
Pointed into the western sun
And in the sand
Skeleton of the leviathan.
She will persist in her desire
Until she, Sacajawea stands, earth's daughter
As waves roll in, the smell of salt
Crash of spray along the coast
She'll hold this always
Confrontation with what can't be mapped
Or ever stilled—
The end of continent
A self of water.

Lewis and Clark

Obliteration of the tribes
Begins with drawing a map on hide
Where distance is marked not by space but by time

Star people have their own migrations
Glaciers can cover half a continent
A planet wobble a sun

Ghost towns inhabited only by the spirit of smallpox
Along the great rivers
The shirt that must protect its wearer

Pipe carved with a crouching figure
Timber, debris, floating downstream
What's random—or purposive

This entire journey essentially about rivers
A waterway that exists only
In an imagined geography

And the mind
Even trained to sextants
And the surveyor's steady thumb against the horizon

Can weaken, reel, despair
The horizon, after all, is a construction
Both an illusion, and in its way

An idea you move towards.

Northwest

The totem pole commemorating atomic energy
Shows the United States as eagle
Russia as an Orthodox priest
Then a man on top of the sun
And Raven, creator, who stole the moon.

The grave marker of a naked woman
Has cannibal breasts
Each with a face—eyes, nose, mouth
Death, you are no child to suck,
Some things will bite back.

These trees that sail their masts into the skies
What shamans climb, stepladder to the North Star
Can fall and rot, become nurse logs
From which sprout
The devil's claw, the fern, the spruce.

Last night I dreamed my own mother
Killed a bear to eat
Hoisted it over her shoulders
Hiked out.
Yes, these woods are that deep.

Sitka

Intense foxgloves
Speckled inside of purple bells,
The Russian orthodox saint
Like digitalis
Stimulates belief.
Things burn—an onion dome, a minaret,
The icon rescued from the flames
Becomes something unscathed in the story.
Beneath the planks of the Siberian house
Permafrost buckles floorboards.
Prisoners freed from the Gulag
Can no longer imagine going home
And so, in the village of carvers
They start to shape bone, ivory,
Fossilized walrus tusk.
A bee can be preserved in amber
So can the heart.
There are swans on the salt estuary
And in the song of betrayal, and in
The story of transformation.
Farther down along the island's coast
Tall poles stand in the cedar and spruce
Where raven might land on the top
And a killer whale swim down
Out of a mouth ringed by suckers or octopus
And a peaked hat
On the seated figure's head
Speaks of congress with the other world.

The Crystal Mask

Blue ice in every shape that nature can arrange—
Grotesque, faery, Steuben, glass-blown
Losing its crystalline azure structure with age

We sit on the sandy beach in middle-age
Admiring this glacier, snow peaks lost in mist
Seeming bigger than the mind

This moment I really don't mind
My hips, my aches and pains, a familiar set
Ice can dissolve, can calve, can replicate

Delicate late arriving orchids on a stem, replicate
By seed, the blue wands of lupine
Like seals or whales, bear the fertile seed within

Casing, nest, a home, mammalian womb within
That calls the dance of bees
Not parthenogenesis, like matreshka wooden dolls

A virgin birth, the stack of nesting dolls
Identical, though all things change
From ice to water in a lake of floating shapes

Icebergs, shining, shaped
Like the Taj Mahal in moonlight
Drifting as we speak out of our warm hands' range.

The Glass Mask

Raven stole the moon
Pearl of blown glass
With a human face

Opening the icon
Is to paint from dark to light
The saint's face—is, is not—your face

Four-thousand-year-old villages
The shaman's thumbless hand
Beyond ordinary grasping

A beard of bees hanging in midair
Forming the four letters
Of the name of God

Raven can turn one thing into another
Raven figured out day follows night
Raven opened stacked cedar boxes to create

The glass mask is both a lie and revelation
The eyes might see you
And yet you are also seeing

Spirit of earthquake woke me
Dreaming of the sea, still I knew
I was not shaking myself awake

Crow is my bird
Bossy, shameless, curious, without remorse
But you already knew that

White lilac,
Dusk . . .

There's no fountain here
In my courtyard
Water falling into a white scallop shell
Just a procession of plastic ducks
Collapsed in a heap
Over the winter

My girl child and a boy
Who will soon be a man
Open the gate
And walk off down the block together

The Spanish word for open
Resonates in my head
The day before my fiftieth birthday
"Abierto"—
Expecting a knock on the door.
You say it still might snow.

"These blue days and this sun of childhood"*

Ellipse of stars, Venus in the west
Over the neighbor's late leafing trees
Wall's peeling stucco
Girls at fifteen
Arms up in the air in tribal bellydance
It is improvised
Although the patterns repeat
Each holds finger cymbals but does not strike
Vowels in the throat ululate.

A melancholy—evening coming on
The poet's last line written coughing in the pensione
Across the border.
In Spanish, Arabic, Greek alphabet—
Hypographic, a ring of feeling
Out of the limbic
A fragment
Written on the back of the hand.

Leafy green vine grows along the wire
A handwritten invitation,
The word watercourse.
How many minutes add up
To years spent washing teaspoons in soapy water,
Sweeping the front porch
With a frayed broom,
Scrubbing the table?
Even the priest with arms uplifted
Could speak of sacrifice
But not tally up
This line's persistence.

*Last line ever written by Antonio Machado, found in his overcoat pocket.

After Pessoa

"To be a poet is not my ambition,
It's my way of being alone"—
Secluded, among a multiplicity of selves
Like the child who traces the vast oriental carpet
With a finger, or who runs the little car model
Along the tendrils and medallions
As if they were the streets of some unknown city.

A mirror is not a window, and yet it might be
A passerby in the window is a fragment
Of the rainy street—one person
Contains the bits of other selves
Like a run-down theater
In a shabby neighborhood
Performing Shakespeare, or Brecht.

Night falls with its algebra
Not just subtraction and division
But the idea that X
Signifies one thing, Y another
Looking for correspondence, still you say
"Nothing returns" in defiance of physics—
And like light, "everything is real."

I'm Looking At Her Too (The Model)

Who walks in in her kimono
Inexpensive, silky, flowered
Carrying her street clothes and sneakers
And suddenly crouches naked
In the middle of the room.
In the gesture drawing
If even the word hip
Or elbow
Comes into your mind
You are drawing too slowly.
But what about desire, pink skin, her ass
And surely flesh is a shock
Even for the surgeon with the knife
Or the young man with the charcoal in his hand
Or the woman drawing, who imitates
This pose—hands on hips, belly forward, coral necklace
And who must eventually cover the blank white page
With a large soft empty circle.

Floating World

You used to call it the floaty life.
Sitting on the porch all summer
Grilling on the little hibachi
Watching the street.
Looking for rain
To flood in silver monsoon.
Our windows covered in rice paper,
A cage full of zebra finches
And the two trees
The irritable landlord planted
One in each little fenced plot
That passed for a front yard
Which I watered with the care
Of a childless woman . . .
We slept on the floor,
Moving the futon from room to room,
Seeking what—
A darker kiss, a lighter dream
The sensation of caravan.

Days went by in a reverie of seeking
Wisdom in the pages of a book.
The fat poet was hungry, and we fed him
Blini with caviar, the big hamburgers
From Dave's Not Here.
And I read, page by page, hour after idle hour.
One afternoon, you came into the sunny living room
And ordered me to move
Surprised, I looked up
Then, seeing your expression

Did as I was told
Left the banco banked by houseplants
Where you darted in and snatched
The boa constrictor—iridescent peacock, mother-of-pearl—
Escaped from its cage of glass.
You said it watched me turn each page
With small glittering eyes, unblinking
Tracking the reader's hand.

We lived, although we scarcely realized it
Two blocks from Witter Bynner's house
Just round the corner, across the street, then left
To where the gracious sprawl of hacienda
Had housed poets, parties
Love affairs, betrayals, the twists and turns
Of hearts by a pueblo deco metal framed window
Or figures dancing on a Chinese screen.

The Japanese color block prints
Show that floating world, or demimonde
Actors, geishas, whores
Out and out criminals and
Writers, poets
A moon, hair framed in a clip
Hand mirror, the street at night . . .
Like lily pads that float on pond scum
Like the pink lotus out of muddy water
This world is our world and also its shadow
Beauty—a commodity—love—a happenstance.

Years later, I'll walk by the place
And think that I might see us there
You in your beard, Phil in a big white T-shirt
And me, the girl
Who doesn't do much of anything
But try to concentrate
And not get caught.
One tree is dead, the other grown
And I've gone on
To find another stoop to sit upon
And watch the rain come on.

Ford

Between West Alameda
And the less obvious East Alameda
The river is flowing high before the falls
After so many years of drought.
You've taken me here because it is simply beautiful
With two folding chairs
And a large purple parasol
To hold over my head.
Brilliant yellow bird—an oriole?—
With blazing orange beak
Flits about
And a young girl, armful of cocker spaniel
Fords the stream.

Nearby in a garden of wind sculptures
Forty or fifty—noiseless
Tulips and flames, double wheels, patterns
Like plains windmills or flocks of birds—
Turn to a music we cannot hear
But rather sense, delicate metal arms and curves
Cast shadows on the gravel path, late afternoon
Changing shapes against the bluest sky
Marked by clouds and contrails.

That ford on the river—
Years ago, before the crossing bridge came down
When water was still something
We took for granted
A turquoise truck tried to take the shortcut home
Instead got stranded in the raging stream,
And the driver and passengers climbed on top
Of the cab above the brown and frothy flood
Waiting for rescue
From all that sudden river.

Mid-Life

The story you've told yourself for so long
Is over—it hasn't ended
Just stopped abruptly.
The bread crumbs that led out of the dark forest
Have been eaten by ravens and crows;
Even if you dropped lovely white stones
They've turned into toadstools.
We're so beyond the wicked stepmother now
The incompetent father, the hunger.
You turn to look in the mirror
And it is the witch's face that looks back at you.
You are no longer the girlchild who survives
On her wits and the language of animals
Now it is your turn to start building
A house that is edible.
Maybe you weren't even lost to begin with
Maybe happily ever after is how the story begins
And the child who is let out of the cage
Who escapes the oven
Says suddenly at the end
Once upon a time.

Heaven and Hell

The kids tell me
There are tunnels beneath the city

Lost cities in the arroyo
Crumbling from abandoned childhood

The lit tunnel is called heaven
The dark one—hell

You can go there
And do anything

Leave behind a foil wrapper
Or a used needle

No one will take me there—
I'll never be sixteen again

Drawing the hopscotch board in chalk
Casting the pebble

Hopping on one foot
From Hell across the numbered board to Paradise

The city appears solid
But the tunnels, they tell me, start near the mall

And aren't we all strangers
Wayfarers, pilgrims . . .

Exile

In Arabic there is one word
That means talking in the dark,
A word associated with love.

Ever since my birth
I've been walking away from a tight place.

Maybe someday I'll leave even this city
And start telling its story.

Notes

"The Dyer's Palmprint." I was inspired by an exhibition of painted textiles from southern Morocco at the Museum of International Folk Art.

"Dar-Al-Islam" is in Abiquiu, New Mexico. Thanks to my brother Daniel Sagan for taking me there.

"Ana Mendieta: Falling in the Four Elements." Ana Mendieta, Cuban-American artist, was a performance artist, sculptor, and part of the first wave of feminist artists. On September 8, 1985, she plunged to her death from the thirty-fourth floor of her Manhattan apartment. Her husband, Carl Andre, the famous minimalist, was tried and acquitted for her murder.

"Emergence." Thanks to Marilyn Batts/Leah Stravinsky for inspiration here.

"Anna Zemánková." I became aware of her work at a show at Santa Fe's Museum of International Folk Art: "Vernacular Visionaries: International Outsider Art." The accompanying book edited by Annie Carlano was of great use.

"Columns." I admired the columns on Baca Street for many years, and when they were taken down I went in search of their origin. Book artist Paula Hocks had memorialized them and claimed that they were originally from the old state Capitol. Valerie Brooker, at the library at the current Capitol, did further research and discovered that they were most likely from the First National Bank. In any case, they and their brethren are gone. Many thanks to Valerie for her enthusiastic response to the "stump the librarian" question.

"Each Thing Has Its Own Meaning." Section 1 was inspired in part by a visit to Baltimore's American Visionary Art Museum. "Bed for Damballah" is a mixed media installation by Nancy Josephson. Holocaust survivor Esther Nisenthal Krinitz (1927–2001) created an entire narrative of her life story in embroidery and fabric collage that is also reminiscent of the tapestries done by refugees from Cambodia. Section 3 draws some of its imagery from multimedia artist Amalia Amaki's exhibit "Boxes, Buttons and the Blues" at the National Museum of Women in the Arts in Washington, DC. It also pays homage to the Quilts of Gee's Bend from Alabama. Thanks to Judith Powsner for taking me to Boston's Museum of Fine Arts to see them.

"Friable" and "You Left" are in memory of my friend Elizabeth Searle Lamb who died in the winter of 2005. She was eighty-eight years old and best known as "the first lady of haiku" in English.

"Dharani of the Return"—A dharani is a magical Buddhist incantation, chanted for the efficacy of its sound.

"Northwest Passage." Thanks to the Jefferson Library at Monticello for help explaining Jefferson's notions that the geologic past potentially still existed in the American West. Some of these phrases were taken directly from journals of the expedition.

"These blue days and this sun of childhood." Antonio Machado (1875–1939), one of the greatest Spanish poets of the twentieth century.

"After Pessoa." Fernando Pessoa (1888–1935), Portuguese poet. The quotation is from *Fernando Pessoa & Co.*, translated by Richard Zenith.

"Ford." Thanks to Hope Atterbury for her gift of these views.